Patricia Mary Finn

C000148947

Divine Realisation

One Soul's Journey

S.O.L BOOKS

Published by: S.O.L. Books, PO Box 280, St. Neots PE19 9ED

It is S.O.L. Books policy to use papers that are natural, renewable and
recyclable products and made from wood grown in sustainable forests.
The logging and manufacturing processes are expected to conform to
the environmental regulations of the country of origin.

ISBN 978-0-9563073-0-9

Produced by S.O.L. Books

Distributed by Troubador Publishing Ltd, 5 Weir Road, Kibworth,
Beauchamp, Leicester LE8 0LQ
Type design & layout by Pentacorbig, High Wycombe
Cover design by Pentacorbig, High Wycombe
Cover Photograph: Rainbows over Rockingham (Ireland) by Ben Millett,
see full version at www.benmillett.com

Printed and bound in the UK by TJ International, Padstow, Cornwall

S.O.L. Books
www.solbooks.co.uk

Contents

Dedication

I take this opportunity to acknowledge the special people in my life, my dear Mother, a kind and giving person who always chose the generous and loving solution to the many tests presented to her in her life, I am proud to be her daughter. My husband Barrie, a patient and gentle man, my beautiful kind-hearted daughter Maria and my deep and quiet son Philip. Also, to all of my grandchildren, who bring me light and joy whilst in their presence, awakening that 'inner child' in me.

I also acknowledge with love my brothers Johnny and Michael and although Michael is no longer with us I know that he watches from afar. To all the special people in my life, thank you for your moral support or your help, you know who you are. Last, but not least, is my dear Father whose departure from this world awakened something inside of me which led me on a fascinating expedition of discovery, I know his love walked beside me through much of that journey, turning the signposts back in the right direction if I started to go down the wrong route, I take this opportunity to say, with eternal Love 'Thank You, Dad'.

Introduction

As I recorded my thoughts in this book I held a picture of my grandchildren in my mind and imagined I was talking to them at a later stage in their lives when they were all 'grown-up', grown-up in mind, body and spirit, enough to stop one day and ask themselves what life was all about.

After my 'transition', I studied many subjects that slowly but surely led me to a profound realisation that there was more to life than I could have ever imagined possible. I had 'climbed out of the box', sat on top and looked in wonder as I saw that waiting for me were the answers to everything about life and beyond. Knowledge is light and with that light comes peace of mind, the greatest gift one can receive and this is what I wish, in whatever small way, to pass on.

My grandchildren may look back and remember my encouragement to treat all others as they wish to be treated regardless of colour, creed or race, this also included guidance for them to respect nature and its creatures as they played in my back garden, 'if you stamp on that snail its mummy and daddy will cry', I would say, looking at them knowingly, or, 'if you don't put that worm back its family will be very sad', this may seem silly or unimportant to some but I believe it nurtures a healthy attitude to everything which has 'life' right down to the plants and trees around us, such guidance does and did seem to make them stop and think about their next move.

I deliberately keep subjects in this little book light rather than cloud the mind with deeper issues relating to our existence as my intent is just to sow a metaphorical seed that may, in time, blossom towards the light.

chapter one

A new world

How did I manage to climb out of the 'box' of life, sit on top, look around and see a new world? When did I realise that my existence was more than just walking, running or stumbling, from one of life's experiences to another? What gave me a sudden unquenchable thirst for knowledge of life itself? How did I discover peace of mind and why do I view people and every day situations so differently now? It all began slowly with the first taste of real sorrow in my life, the loss of a loved one. Something within me started to awaken, a door was opened, and I walked through to embark upon a search for the key to open the next doorway, behind which stood my own personal Holy Grail.

When I bothered to think about it, I thought life was just about going through all the 'ages and stages' and then dying. That was all there was, over and out!

Yes, I had heard of heaven or hell, where we were meant to go depending on how we are in this life, but although, as explained later, I knew about it through the faith of my birth, the reality of it did not warrant my full attention. I was too busy living day to day, with worldly worries and my busy 'monkey chatter mind' to keep me company.

I lived within my family circle, being happy with the company of loved ones and friends but over the many years I also walked through many difficult encounters, in my personal and working life. I faced tests that pulled me headlong through a hedgerow of emotions leaving me mentally shattered, my faith in fellow humans taken to the limit many times.

One day a close family member said 'Patricia, you don't laugh anymore', I was shocked at this innocent statement, particularly when I realised it was true. Where had my spirit gone; where was the laughing child who ran around the fields of her grandfather's farm in Ireland looking under stones and rocks for fairies (only to find frogs!); at what point along the way did I lose myself; when did I stop laughing and when did I start taking life so seriously that it effected the very essence of who I was, casting a cloud over the lightness I had known in my younger years ?

At one time, whilst mentally struggling to cope with people and pressures, I reasoned that it would be prudent to find the gift of a thick skin, not caring anymore, letting difficulties go over my head and I became determined to look beyond any problem, but this did not work, it was not 'me', every upset was taken

4

to heart and would wake me up at night to haunt me.

I didn't realise it then, but I realise it now, that I was lost in the corridors of my own mind giving too much thought and energy to things that had not one iota of importance to my existence as an individual soul. One day my life changed forever and in the process of that change I gathered enough strength of mind and purpose to take the first step on a path that would lead me to a place in the highest part of my mind, from this vantage point I could suddenly see the reason for it all, the bigger picture, my past sensitivities became lost in the beauty of what I saw.

The formative years

My Irish mother gave birth to me on St. Patrick's Day in Honeypot Lane Hospital, Kingsbury, North London and both of my parents worked hard to provide a good future for my two older brothers and myself. I was brought up surrounded by the love, not only of my parents but of my grandparents, aunts, uncles and cousins, they were and (*those still with us*) are still loving and giving with hearts of gold. Mind you, the odd 'thump' by one of my two brothers would serve to 'ground' me, keeping me in touch with reality! This start in life was a blessing but it did not prepare me for the world that waited for me.

The early summers of my childhood were spent laughing and running through the fields on my grandfather's farm in Ireland, playing hide and seek with my brothers around the bright yellow gorse bushes, feeding the chickens, looking for fairies, or listening to the echoes coming back to us when we shouted into the air behind the big brick grain store opposite my grandparents white-stoned cottage. Life was freedom and fun, no worries or cares, just the beauty of nature all around us.

Following the family faith I was duly sent to two Catholic schools: St. Bernadette's and St. Gregory's in Kenton, Harrow, and to Pitman's College in Wembley, North London.

I travelled through my teenage days as a 'sixties' girl, one minute in a black-and-white dress, white boots and lashings of black eye make-up, the next following the trend to be one of the 'Flower People', flowered suit, flower in my hair, small bell around my neck! I was also a 'Mod' (as opposed to a 'Rocker') with cropped hair and a paisley suit, dancing to Motown music as part of the audience on *Ready, Steady Go*, the top pop television programme of its day. In our 'Mod' outfits my friend Anita and I appeared on *Ready Steady Go* twice, once dancing on the stage with the Four Tops. I remember the manager at my workplace coming into the office the next day saying 'I don't know, I sit here all day looking at you and then I go home, switch on the television and there you are again!' Heady, fun days indeed.

Up until I left home to get married, I went to church every Sunday without fail even though I suffered from a form of claustrophobia, regularly fainting in the aisle as I tried to get out into the fresh air. Once I even fainted at the feet of a handsome boy I had noticed on my way into the church, finding he had mysteriously disappeared when I eventually regained consciousness (and my dignity!)

In leaving the influence of my family I turned my back on the religion of my birth; somewhere inside of me I did not accept the 'fear factor', which was prevalent in the sermons of that time. God was painted as wrathful, ruling by threats of hell and damnation if you didn't do as 'He' commanded, it didn't seem like a very loving God to me and I didn't particularly want the negativity of the 'fear' emotion in my life. however, I still respected the faith but made a conscious choice not to follow it any longer.

I am at a stage now where I remain forever grateful for the introduction to the concept of faith, the grounding given was a good anchor for me, even if I reeled that anchor up and sailed away, lost in the seas of life; at least I had it there to lower again, this time firmly and permanently in the unyielding fabric of my being.

After my 'transition' I actually started to comprehend the real meanings behind the lessons taught and through my own studies I discovered my own truth about life itself and beyond. A realisation blossomed in my mind that all is not as it seems and there is so much more to life than I had formally believed.

In my search for 'Truth' it also gradually dawned on me that there actually is a Higher Power, a Divine Being; any existence of doubt that I may have formally harboured in the back of my mind vanished. I had been asleep in this world not knowing or caring about anything beyond the life I was living. For the want of a better phrase, I shall call the change in my perception 'an awakening', it was a measured happening over many years where little by little I could begin to see through the shadows, something inside of me turned and gave a wide smile of welcome.

Thank You

Thank you God for Life and Love,
for the beauty all around,
I've spent too many years
with my eyes fixed on the ground.

What I did not realise
was the love that's there to find;
I lived within the limitations
of my busy spinning mind.

One day I took a step back,
held my head up, looked around,
the cobwebs fell down from my eyes,
real life is what I found.

The sky, the grass, the flowers,
bright rainbows with sunshine,
simple walks and simple pleasures,
I know they can be mine.

The woodlands and the wildlife,
stars that wink and send their light,
deep blue seas that wave emotions,
morning sunrise, moonlit nights.

The sounds you send around us,
bumblebees and feathered friends,
whispering leaves and running water,
Nature's love, which you extend.

Dear God I want to thank you,
I see the beauty all around.
In this lifetime I have everything,
Heaven on Earth is what I've found.

– Patricia M Finn

chapter two

The transition

My world shifted in the years following my father's death in 1995: at this time I found it difficult to adjust to the knowledge that I would never see him again. At first I continued day to day in a daze of disbelief, adopting a role of strength and immersing myself in the arrangements for his funeral, I was strong, strong for my mother.

Inwardly I lived through the many faces of grief, travelling through each separate emotion: denial, anger, depression and, some time later, acceptance. On the surface I was relatively calm but how I felt inside can only be described in this way: had I been dragged across a field of broken glass I could not have hurt more, it was not a physical or mental pain, it was an ache which seemed to be lodged somewhere deep within my soul.

A fear also gripped me one day that somehow I would forget the memories that had been created with my father in bygone years, I had to record them in case they vanished so I sat at my computer spilling everything out of my mind on to the screen, from my first memories to the last, sometimes running back to the computer to tap in anything I may have forgotten about which had suddenly struck me, memories such as:

- His laughing eyes behind the white beard of the Father Christmas outfit as he pulled presents out of a big red sack. 'One for Johnny, one for Michael and one for Patricia', he would say, as I cowered nervously under a blanket, asking for 'Daddy'. (*'He's making Father Christmas a cup of tea', my mother would say!*)

- Watching his big strides as I walked beside him as a child, holding his hand tightly and trying hard to keep in step. (*I've walked quickly ever since and now others find it hard to keep up!*)

- The Sunday mornings I would go with him to a wholesale warehouse near Petticoat Lane market in London to help select prizes for a charity bingo my father ran for the church.

- The chocolate-coloured puppy he bought me (*much to the dismay of my mother who ended up looking after it!*).

- Those special moments when I waltzed around the ballroom with him on St. Patrick's day, after the Irish Guards band had played Happy Birthday to me, at one of the many dinner and dances my mother and father took me to in London as I grew older.

After spending hours looking through boxes, tins and albums of old photographs of my mother and father, I also created a special photograph album for my mother, in year order, displaying the special moments they had spent together throughout their marriage. The last photograph I placed in the album was one of my father leaning happily against the rails on a ship, smiling at the camera; I felt this depicted him sailing away from us into the distance, but still happy.

In the early days after my father's passing I couldn't understand how the world just continued as though nothing had happened: the sun still came out each morning (it was July!), the birds still sang at dawn, the high street in my local market town was busy with people, as usual, didn't they know or sense that something had changed? In seeing nothing change, I did, slowly, unconsciously and unknowingly. I had no choice but to keep striding forward, day-to-day, until divine intervention stepped in.

Divine intervention

I didn't deliberately set out to learn anything, nor did I set out to find solace in hope, but in the years following my father's passing, I started to stumble across books and studies which would slowly highlight subjects I would never have given house room to before.

In bookstores books seemed to pop up in front of me, drop on the floor or be the only one positioned so that I could not possibly miss it, this sounds crazy but it is true.

My first 'push' on to my future path of discovery happened quite innocently in a shopping mall in Florida whilst I was on holiday in 1997. I was browsing through books in a bookstore and picked up a small book called *Embraced by the Light* by Betty J. Eadie. I flicked through it, read a couple of sentences and put it back continuing to look for new romantic novels, which I was into at the time; this strange book didn't fit the bill. That night I tossed and turned in bed, something in my mind kept nagging me to go back and get that book, it was an inconvenient thought as we had no intention of re-visiting the same shopping mall, but the next morning I just had to go back; there was no sane reason for this sudden desire but I rushed into the shop worried that the book would be gone. Of course it was still there, I read it and the seed was planted.

It is interesting to note that thereafter I never knowingly picked up a book based on fiction, if a book wasn't shining light in some area of my soul or teaching me something I would not read it.

Another very early book 'staring at me' so to speak, was called *Conversations with God* by Neale Donald Walsch, a book and series of books which I eventually found had helped many people through difficult times, in the process also rekindling an interest and curiosity in God; it was God from another angle. Other books I fell across led me to study differing religions, philosophy, geology, biology, quantum physics, near death experiences (*an experience my father had once after an operation*), the power of the sub-conscious mind and many other connected subjects that I still find fascinating.

Whilst reading or studying various books I remained consciously sceptical. I am not prone to believing everything I read, but I developed a personal gauge and sharp gut instinct as to what represented truth or the basis of truth and what did not. Apart from gut instinct, it is difficult to explain how my gauge worked, however, the nearest I can explain it is if the book contained the essence of love throughout, I gave it consideration and due attention, if there was any element of fear or negativity, I threw it over my shoulder, so to speak.

Retaining an open mind was and remains an important ingredient to assessing what is real knowledge for the enquiring mind, truth can be recognised through the heart and, our most powerful guide, intuition.

In the books that I accepted I experienced 'light bulb' moments where my heart recognised the words and smiled, it was not a case of my mind wanting to believe something, it was as if I already knew what I was reading. One of the many sayings that came into my mind (*duly recorded in a little a note book, which I kept close to me to record my ever-flowing thoughts*) was, 'We live life as though we are on the edge of a dream we can't remember'. What I read was like a 'remembering'.

I remained and still remain discerning but I grew in realisation that there are some facts of life that are very difficult to explain but which are very real when you look closer at the subject. Eventually everything suddenly seemed to make sense; everything, right down to the words of the old hymn *Amazing Grace*, '…I once was lost but now I'm found, was blind but now I see'.

Gradually, I discovered a faith within me that is so strong that I often said, to those who would understand, that I could 'walk through a wall with it'. I felt an inner powerhouse driving me forward until I found and 'believed' in the God, the Source, the Creator, who had been waiting patiently for me all along, waiting for me to 'see' that I was not just an inconsequential cog in the wheel of life, waiting for me to see that we all have a purpose to our existence which is far removed from the purpose I formally gave it, waiting for me to see that everything on earth and everybody is important and each has a role to play.

This new-found God did not strike fear into my soul, only I could put that emotion there; I had the power to accept fear or reject it. This God was certainly not the one of my youth, wrathful and demanding, this God was/is one of perfect love, no threats, just gentle guidance sent through many messengers to help us to find our way back to our real home, which is where we all belong, but it is a long arduous journey through many 'dangers, toils and snares'.

Along the way I also developed a deep respect and love for Jesus, a master teacher of life, his words had

16

previously seemed to be trapped within a type of holy mystery of unfamiliar words, but when the essence and meaning were unravelled and seen through the eyes of the heart, all became clear.

Mentally, a lightness of thought settled in my mind and I began to express my newfound beliefs, feelings and dreams through simple poetry, which I recorded mainly for my own reflection. Family members started to ask for copies, so I made bookmarks out of them and the positive quotations I had collected and created along the way. My work is now displayed on my website and the address for this is www.divinerealisation.co.uk. (*I have also included some of my poems within this book at the end of most chapters.*)

I remember feeling a real sense of achievement when my website was launched, mainly because I had managed to include every colour of the rainbow in its design. My family and friends know how much I love rainbows, I'm not sure why, but when I see one over a nearby field or anywhere on my travels, I experience a great sense of joy, my eyes light up at the beauty of the colours, for me the rainbow is one of nature's most magical gifts, indeed a reminder of the wonders this earth has to offer.

Full circle

I felt that I needed to channel my new-found belief, but how? I then made a conscious decision to re-adopt the faith of my birth, I knew that I would now understand

and actually enjoy the energy of the services I had formally found boring and inconsequential to my life.

I was initially wary of returning to 'religion', it had been given a bad name along the way, but I knew that this time it would be on my terms, my mind remaining freethinking and unfettered by any constraints it may have tried to throw around me in former years. It was a relief and refreshing to find that gone were the 'hell and brimstone' sermons, in their place were teachings of optimism and love that I could now appreciate in a new light of understanding.

In returning to church, I not only found the existence of a beautiful energy, created by prayers and blessings over many years, I also found a place where there were many good people, kind people, people who are on a similar wavelength. My decision to channel my newfound beliefs back to familiar territory does not separate me from the knowledge that there are many good people who choose not to follow a 'set' path; they hold their own faith in whatever way they choose. Keeping an open mind and an open heart is an essential ingredient to life. Had I not kept my mind open, I would not have gained the knowledge that I have to date, such knowledge going beyond the boundaries of religion. Had I not kept my heart open I would not have found my own truth, nor would I have touched and aligned with the deep knowing within me, a deep knowing that exists within everyone.

I remain curious, asking questions to enable me to embrace truth and reject distortion as they make appearances along the path of my journey. I am seeking and I am still finding.

Over the last ten years I have seen a major shift in the acceptance of subjects that formally did not put in an appearance on the world's stage, such subjects now being covered in the spiritual section of every book store I know. Formally there was no spiritual section containing the number of books available now, so the shift is observable. We also have well-known personalities such as Oprah Winfrey, a highly evolved soul who is walking her walk and bringing understanding of the many subjects attached to the meaning of our lives into the homes of the general public.

One of my findings is that the more I learn, the more there is to learn, there seems no end and there are so many attached subjects, I'm not sure my thirst will ever be quenched. However, I am grateful that I found that switch in my mind which sent me off on a fascinating adventure, one which I wish to share with you, dear reader.

As mentioned in the Introduction, I am not going to cover everything I have picked up along the way, I am merely covering 'lighter' subjects which are based on my own personal understanding of them, some information may seem far-fetched or difficult to understand by those who do not yet understand, but I only ask you to consider my findings and ask yourself 'what if this is all true?'

Maybe, dear reader, you will concur with some of it, all of it or none of it, this is your choice; I do not seek to change anyone's perception, I am merely reflecting my own. There are many who have already made their own journey, but if you haven't maybe one day you will choose to embark on a personal voyage of discovery taking whichever path suits you as an individual and, like me, along the way you will pick up a bright light that you can use to shine on any darkness you encounter. This light will also guide you towards understanding who you are, why you are here and where you are going.

If you have no interest in the thought of anything connected with the meaning of life, at this time, or of the existence of a higher power, look away now; for the reader who is curious, take my hand and follow me on a journey through my thoughts and let me show you what I have found.

Beacon of Light

I would like to be a Beacon
of Light out in the sea,
so all the ships lost in the dark
could find their way to me.

Steer their craft along the waves,
light up the sky above,
show them Truth & Hope & Faith,
introduce our God of Love

For fellow man for planet earth,
for all things great and small,
untie the ropes, cast out their nets,
teach equality for all.

Their lives would then be happy,
their hearts would be full too,
and if they start to weaken,
they would know just what to do

Unfurl their sails, steer out again
for the Beacon that they know
(it's really there within their hearts,
they won't have far to go!).

– Patricia M Finn

*My Parents,
John and Mary*

*A short break from
running free on my
Grandfather's farm aged 3*

*In a park in
Dollis Hill, London
with my brothers
Johnny & Michael*

*A family 'fun' day out
at the seaside with my
brothers and Mother*

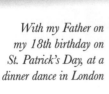

*A 'Twiggy' pose
in my Flower Power days*

*With my Father on
my 18th birthday on
St. Patrick's Day, at a
dinner dance in London*

chapter three

The meaning of life (part 1)

Where do I start on a topic that is so vast? In reality I have only scratched the surface of this subject and I still have many questions whirring around within my mind. However, slowly I am finding that my questions are being answered, with the answers coming at a time when I am mentally evolved enough to be receptive for the new truths.

To begin to understand what life is all about, the first thing needed is the knowledge that we all have a higher self, an inner self, a bright shining energy that lives within each one of us, an energy which is more than our human minds can completely comprehend. That energy is a type of consciousness, which is who we really are; we each have this energy of consciousness and it is eternal, not just for this moment in time. We are not our body; the body is purely a vehicle for the energy which, for the sake of brevity, I will call the soul from hereon in. Jesus tried to tell us this, 'The Kingdom of God is within you', a saying which is not often understood.

In biology and quantum physics it is known that invisible energies that are constantly spinning and vibrating exist, atoms are like wobbly spinning tops that radiate their own identifying energy patterns, so everything in the universe including you and me, radiates a unique energy signature; we are vibrational transmitters and receivers.

The atom has no physical structure; it is made out of invisible energy not tangible matter. An excellent book to read on this subject is *The Biology of Belief* by Bruce H. Lipton a well-known cell biologist whose groundbreaking research has uncovered a link between life and consciousness. Gregg Braden is a New York Times best-selling author who also explores miracles that are available in the quantum world, and how knowledge of them can help each one of us.

Some people will only believe in what they can 'see', a bit like the 'Flat Earth' Society that believed there was nothing over the horizon because they couldn't see it. Logically this doesn't make sense as we are surrounded by many things we cannot see from the cells in our own bodies, radio/cellular waves, to the air we breath, we can only see the affects of these things so it stands to reason that there is much more.

Returning to the existence of the energy within us and around us, our souls, how many people really look at themselves in a mirror, stare into their eyes and wonder how they can function as a person with just a body, a grey mass called a brain and our nervous system, animals have the same but they do not function at the same level.

So, why are we here? In short, 'Life is a schoolroom' and we are here to learn lessons. We are here to remember the truth of who we are, as created by the source from whence we came, God (*yes, there is a God/Creator/Higher power which I will cover later*), in order to become a better version of ourselves, to grow and evolve in knowledge and spiritual awareness, enough to recognise right from wrong and enough to overcome every difficulty we face with strength and, where necessary, detachment.

Repetition is good so I will repeat the statement, 'we are here to become a better version of ourselves, to grow and evolve in knowledge and spiritual awareness'. We are also here to help others as we grow in knowledge. As we climb that ladder we look behind us and offer a hand to those below us, whilst grasping the hand of those above us, so, we are all linked together although we cannot see this, we feel we are separate but we are not, our fellow 'being' is also on a journey, whatever that journey is for them.

The respect for each individual's right to choose their own path, whether we believe it is right or wrong is what we have to accept, we are not here to cast judgement, everyone perceives life in a different way, but we need to be aware that we all come from the same Source.

Some people think that the tests we face in life and situations presented to us are 'normal', but normal is the fact that we are born to be happy and the bright inner light is only dimmed by either the negative conditioning and programming received in childhood – which can be changed – or the workings of our own minds. We build our own cages and only we can open the door.

The main aim of our journey is to find and listen to our inner wisdom, face and learn the lessons and arrive at a platform where we 'choose' to work towards removing the obstacles that hold us back from progressing, such obstacles being the ones we place in our minds, giving more energy and attention to them than we should.

Life is also how we deal with the lessons and difficulties presented to us, these ultimately display who we are as a person and ultimately as an individual soul. We each have our own lessons to learn, we can't ask anyone what ours are, they are all different lessons and in our hearts we know what they are.

Each individual person is responsible for making choices in their lives. We can choose to be kind or cruel, giving or selfish, generous or miserly, compassionate or judgemental, forgiving or vengeful; we have the capacity to follow the light within us or the darkness, it is a battleground and it is we who choose and create who we are, not anybody else.

One of life's biggest challenges is to overcome

weaknesses in behaviour or character; recognising our weaknesses is the first step. Masters of life have learned how to detach from the importance we put on our egos, for example, how strong are we when we are insulted by others. This is the test of patience, our humility is tested by the proud, our faith by the unfaithful, our hope by the person who has no hope, justice by the unjust, gentleness and kindness by the cruel. Other people are the channel through which we are all tested.

A major weakness in life is that many people worry too much about what other people think of them. This doesn't mean we need not treat everyone with respect, be dignified or operate outside of what others feel, but we need more focus on what we think of ourselves. We are not here to impress others, we come into this life alone and we leave alone, alone with what we have achieved as a soul in this lifetime, what vices we managed to overcome and which virtues we managed to adopt.

Apart from love and the good deeds we create, which rest in our souls, we don't take any of those material things we have owned, struggled and worked hard for, we take nothing but ourselves. Yes, work with others, give to others, help others (*for we are also here to help those souls who are in need of our help*), love others, have fun with others this is also part of life but along the way we have to look to ourselves to see if we 'like' who we are or who we have become. *Also, hold the thought that if our love for others is dependent on attitudes and feelings towards us, it is not love.*

It does help soul progression to mix with people on the same soul wavelength, as the soul develops it is more likely that we will feel more comfortable and able to learn more with people who share our views and understandings. Where possible, it is best to avoid people whose view on life is based on negativity, they can be energy 'vampires' soaking up any lightness we have, leaving a cloud of darkness in its place.

We are total masters and creators of our 'You'niverse and we can break harmful habits and replace them with something better by thinking higher thoughts, thinking beauty, love, forgiveness, optimism and thinking truth, banishing negative ways and thoughts striving to become more aware of our potential as a divine being. We are sparks of 'the Higher Power', our Creator made us in His likeness and we have to strive to throw off the illusion that we are less than this, like a caterpillar emerging from it's cocoon, we have it within our capabilities to find out just how beautiful we are, if we choose to. Real beauty is not external, it is internal.

Our life is led by our perception of it; we all hold different views on everything and everyone. If we wish to open that 'cage door' we have shut behind us we can work to change any negativity we have adopted. A good teaching book I found is *A Course in Miracles* by The Foundation for Peace. When I first heard of this book I thought to myself, *'Goody, learn how to do the odd miracle, that will come in handy!!'*,but the course is on something more, it is a course on how to change our negative perceptions and in doing so we can change our minds and therefore our lives, that is the miracle.

If we had a blessed life, sitting on the beach every day knocking the odd coconut out of the tree, what a waste of a life that would be. What would we learn? It is said that those with the most difficult lives are the most blessed as they are learning more than others, a difficult concept to understand and I still have much to learn on this one, but I do know there are many emotions we have to learn to conquer, to become master of and not a victim.

It takes special soul courage to face the dragon (the emotion), master it, detach from its claw finding peace in conquering something that no longer has the power to hurt or affect your life. Being the master of your mind and hormones and not letting them be master of you is the warrior status we have to achieve, a fight worth winning.

Negative emotions

An example of mastering our minds is to take a negative emotion that we hold on a situation or person and shine some light on it, decide to look at it in a positive way instead, refusing to let the shadows of the bad thoughts dwell in the dark caverns of our minds, drag it out into the light and do not let it return, smile at it, love it, control it for if we don't it will settle, fester and expand.

Like attracts like, for sure, there is a magnetic energy we can create around us that brings this truth into being, so nurturing negativity of any kind will also serve as a magnet for more of the same in our lives, this works on the cosmic 'cause and effect syndrome', which takes our thoughts, words and actions and returns them to us in like form.

We have all come up against people and situations that have caused us mental anguish, sometimes coming into our lives to test us to the limit of our endurance. But is it worth allowing that situation or person to exist in our minds, churning us up, is it worth giving it houseroom when the only thing we should be focused on is the positive things that surround us? It is merely an inconvenient moment, albeit upsetting, in our travels though life and eternity, we can draw on the reserves of self-belief and strength that we have available within us to look through the test, for we are stronger than the emotion we are experiencing and it cannot defeat us, unless we consciously allow it to. Life is about the choices we make, so we can choose to turn our back on any smouldering darkness and keep the light shining brightly in our minds, with awareness and practice we can truly become masters of 'light' refusing to let darkness into our lives, thinking around it, above it and through it.

When I experienced someone or something which had upset me and it was flitting in and out of my mind, I would find a quiet moment to use the powers of my imagination and bring it to the surface. I would visualise it as a picture of the person or the scenario involved that was connected to me by a piece of string, imagine picking up a giant pair of scissors and cutting the string (the thought), then watch as it floated away into the distance, releasing myself from the power that emotion had on me. The small amount of time it takes to release a negative revolving thought is worth it as it is a strong declaration to our sub-conscious minds that we no longer wish the thought to exist.

How do we act when faced with actions or words based on envy, spite or hatred? Can we detach ourselves from the power we allow someone else to have when they aim their own negative emotions at us? It is tempting, but a weakness, to feed bad behaviour with its mirror image, instead accept that we can afford to stand back, so to speak, and rest in the knowledge that bad behaviour never goes unpunished; we do not have to stand and fight our corner.

We are 'energy' and everything in life is energy like a matrix, vibrating at differing frequencies in different locations and levels. Everything we think, say and do is that energy, so when we focus our attention on something we vibrate that signal outward. Any wrongdoing is dealt with in this way, in reality we sin against ourselves and if we go through a run of negative actions or thinking, we will find it is returned to us in many ways. 'What goes around, comes around' is a great universal truth.

So it is true – 'what you give, you will receive' – if you want love, give love; if you want generosity, be generous; if you want kindness, be kind; if you want respect, give respect; if you want friendship, be a friend, and so on. Be the first to do it and do it without expectation, build up a glowing energy and create a loving aura around you, this will slowly but surely attract positive responses into your life.

It is a fact of life that we all make mistakes; in recognising and admitting them we are displaying true strength of character. We are human, we just have to know and accept that mistakes are there to give us a greater understanding of life; they are there for us to learn by, blossom and grow.

Some may choose to take the easy route by blaming others for their mistakes, situation or for the way they think. This is an excuse that weakens the will, each of us has an independent soul, we have an inner power we can utilise to climb out of any black hole we find ourselves in. This is our life, our journey and looking to other people to either blame or hang on to is not going to help our personal evolvement as a soul.

If we rely on others in our lives to provide us with happiness we are being untrue to ourselves. We just need to know that everything we desire in life, all the love, wisdom, power, knowledge, understanding, compassion and all the strength actually resides within us.

As already mentioned, we have to find and look for a way of tapping into what we already have, many strong souls, such as Nelson Mandela, have found this power to draw on and survive even in the darkest hour; when we are at the bottom of a well, there is only one way to look and that is up, with enough willpower we can start climbing up the sides of the well, using the strength of the emotions of fear, anger or despair that we had formally placed there, as stepping stones back towards the light.

Forgiveness

Forgiveness is a potent balm to use when we have been hurt by another, it soothes our souls and minds, and forgiving that person that 'did us wrong' dissipates the poison that seeps into our minds when we hold a grudge, nursing that memory within us.

Forgiveness is the golden key to unlock negative emotions against another, it does not let the other person off the hook and it does not condone what has happened, it heals 'you'. Each time we fester on something we are nurturing it, helping it to grow, spreading its power until eventually it has to manifest in some way, usually as an illness sooner or later in life.

I watched a recent television programme where the mother of a young boy who had been murdered told the interviewer that she had 'forgiven' the person who had committed the crime. She was asked how she could do this and her reply was that she had to deal with the many faces of the deep grief she felt, if she had to deal with the emotions of anger, hate and revenge as well it would be too much for her to bear, so she chose to forgive and focused instead on compassion for the parents of the murderer who were suffering too.

There is a potent power in forgiveness, indeed when native American Indians were dying they used to call back their spirits by consciously forgiving all hurts and wrong-doings they had experienced in their life-time, at the same time also recognising and forgiving themselves for any wrongdoing they had created. I have learned that this kind of act is important to do before leaving this existence, carrying any darkness in our souls when we pass on will prevent us getting to where we want to go.

Where it is possible it is better to practice detachment and detachment does take practice; it doesn't come easily when we have been immersed and led by our emotions all of our lives. As we get older we get better at hiding our true feelings, but if a situation or person's behaviour goes deep into our being it will live there, quite comfortably, resting at the back of our subconscious. We may think we've buried the problem, long 'got over it', but have we?

Compassion is one of the most important emotions to connect with to achieve a deeper understanding of life, whether it is for people or any other form of life on this planet.

When observing the world around us, a connection with the compassion we hold can be made if we look at everything and everybody through the eyes of our hearts, we will then see a different world. When daily life brings us in contact with those who appear to behave badly or in a negative fashion, whether it is an angry motorist overtaking us at speed, a rude person pushing past us in a queue, a surly check-out person at our local supermarket, grumpy or pessimistic people or neighbours, accept that they all have their story to tell. We do not know what hides behind some behaviour or the history of it, we do not know what troubles are spinning around in their minds, we have not 'walked ten miles in their shoes'. We are surrounded by fellow souls who are on their own journey and I'm sure we have all had 'bad days' where our minds are locked into either some kind of emotional stress or negative thought patterns. We are not here to judge anyone but ourselves. Rest easy in the knowledge that extreme cases of bad behaviour are dealt with by the 'cause and effect' syndrome I mentioned earlier.

Loving thy neighbour

Loving thy neighbour is something else to address and in earlier days I couldn't grasp what this meant, surely you can't love other people in the same way you love those closest to you? What did it mean? I found that the 'love' mentioned isn't a literal term; it doesn't mean the kind of love that is extended to family.

Like a diamond, love has many facets and comes in many colours, each is good, for example you may love your partner in a different way to your child, your mother in a different way to your sister or brother, and so on. Giving love to a stranger is done through the facets of acceptance, respect and the practice of treating others as you wish to be treated, one of the most important aspects of human existence to 'do unto others as you wish to be done unto you', helping them if they need help, regardless of colour, creed or race.

37

In my studies on differing faiths I found that they basically all have the same teachings, the paths may be different but the goals are the same, whether it is Christianity, Islam, Hinduism, Buddhism, Judaism, Confucianism, Taoism, and so on. They all have a golden rule within each, set out in differing contexts, but all meaning the same and that is the need for followers to 'treat all others as they wish to be treated'.

What a wonderful world we would live in if everybody followed the guidance given through many sources, helping each other, looking out for each other, no metaphorical walls where people from different towns, cities, states, countries were treated as 'aliens' from another planet; they would be treated with respect and kindness. There would be no need for the sceptre of 'difference' to wave its mighty sword, casting a shadow over those souls who cannot see we are all the same with the same emotions. Walls would come tumbling down with the energy of love dissolving the fear-based derision which some apply to 'anything or anyone different', whether it is the colour of their skin, their religious views or even the opposing football team: how small we can be!

Charity

Where does charity stand? Yes, many of us respond to charitable organisations or to a beggar we may pass on the street: it feels good to give and so it is. Charity given with compassion is light to the soul, charity that is given for effect or to impress others is not recognised nor registered by our own souls as it is not 'real', it is an act of our egos, one of the biggest weaknesses we are here to overcome. If we could live life through our hearts and not our egos we would have found valuable nourishment for our spiritual growth.

It is important to accept that our own inner soul knows exactly whether our positive actions are based on falseness, pretence or truth; we can fool others but we cannot fool our true selves and as mentioned earlier, it is our own true selves we need to be focused on, not what other people think of us.

The playground

What about enjoying the pleasures in life? There are many positive pleasures to enjoy, life does allow us out of the schoolroom into the playground where pleasures can be as wonderful as we want to make them. There was a Greek philosopher, Epicurus, who divided pleasures into two categories: the noble pleasures and the harmful pleasures, he saw the harmful pleasures as those for which we have to pay a very high price, the sacrifice of our physical health and our peace of mind. He said there is no pleasure in the world which is worth our physical health and peace of mind.

Epicurus described the second category of pleasures as what he called the noble pleasures, the enjoyment of beautiful things in nature: a beautiful sunrise, sunset, the ocean, the mountains, the sky full of clouds, travel, love, good books, good music; his wisdom and philosophy consist of a practical program of living, gradually replacing all our wrong pleasures with the right ones.

Medicine for inner happiness
(Take one a day)

Consider the choices in life and
follow your heart

♥

Nothing can upset you unless you
choose to let it

♥

Look for the beauty in all

♥

Move through your problems
don't live in them

♥

Practice forgiveness and heal yourself

♥

Accept positivity, reject negativity

♥

Make peace with all imperfections

♥

Choose being kind over being right

♥

Accept mistakes as stepping
stones to wisdom

♥

Listen to your feelings
they are usually right

♥

Let others have the glory

♥

Respect all others no matter
what the perceived differences

♥

Always keep an open mind and an open heart

– Patricia M Finn

chapter four

The meaning
of life (part 2)

Daily worries are worries of our mind only, our soul doesn't worry, it knows that day to day concerns will not effect its eternal existence; it just sits and waits patiently for its presence to be recognised and uncovered from the cloak of forgetfulness wrapped tightly around it.

To reiterate, we are all born with an inner light that is more powerful than I could possibly explain. I have found that a tool to use to get some understanding of the power of our inner self and consciousness is meditation, a practice I formally thought was for eastern religions or Buddhist monks, but meditation is becoming more and more popular and part of everyday life for many people. The biblical saying 'Be still and know God' reflects a deep truth and hints at how to find our true selves and from there, peace. Meditation is certainly a peaceful tool. In fact some doctors and studies recommend it for dealing with high blood pressure, stress and other conditions where we need to calm our systems down.

The mind and any out-of-control negative thoughts are the enemy; in reality we have to go 'out of our minds' to find the oasis of peace which exists inside each one of us, the peace that is who we really are.

I would challenge those that do not believe in any higher power, energy or the presence of something extraordinary within him or herself to take a course on meditation with a reputable teacher; their minds will be opened to levels of consciousness they never knew existed.

For those who are interested in meditation the alternative to finding a teacher is to teach yourself, buy a self-help book which will tell you everything you need to know and/or purchase one of the many guided meditation CDs that are available in the shops now. Generally they consist of beautiful calming music with an instructor guiding you into and out of a light meditation.

Meditation is the art of shutting all worldly thoughts out of our minds and it does take practice, it is not easy to stop that 'monkey chatter' mind, but it can be done and the peace that descends to replace the tension in our poor fraught minds is well worth the effort. Just remember, 'Happiness is the space between two thoughts!'

The ideal would be to eventually develop a daily habit of meditating for at least 20 minutes each morning; you will then walk on pink clouds throughout the rest of the day! I remember once waking up, after a restless night, in a high state of anxiety, wound up by worries and events at my workplace. I knew I was teetering on the edge of swirling negative emotions so I decided to take control and gather them up before they swept me away. I went to the bathroom, locked the door, sat on a little seat and meditated for a short while; when I came out of the bathroom I was a completely different woman to the one who had gone in, my prior anxiety had disappeared and I exuded a feeling of peace and calm, which was my companion throughout the rest of the day. I can thoroughly recommend meditation to those who wish to make peace with any worries or negative emotions, it is also excellent for anyone who has a creative mind as space is provided and new, fresh, inspiring thoughts and ideas will fill that space

Yes, meditation brings harmony and clarity of thought, introducing us to the existence of something very potent within ourselves; it is like a kiss to the soul and a blessing for our health, for it is true, the more peaceful we become the longer we will live.

Subconscious Mind

'As a man thinketh, so he is', Jesus taught, and this is so true. As already mentioned, thoughts are energy which get transferred to the subconscious which plays out those thoughts in your life. Henry Ford said 'If you think you can, you're right; if you think you can't, you're right'.

Our subconscious mind is part of who we are as well, this is a mostly unknown, unsung part of us which unconsciously acts like a giant reel-to-reel recorder, recording everything that passes through our minds, every thought, every word and every deed. It does not distinguish between good and bad, spewing out crazy mixed-up thoughts through our dreams. For example, something you may have given just a passing thought to, or a fleeting glance can become the star of your dream, good or not so good, somewhere the subject has registered in the subconscious even if we didn't realise it had.

I used to wonder about the practice of repeating mantras or affirmations, but I have found that positive words that are repeated create a positive energy field around us and they can impact on our sub-conscious minds. For example, if you are anxious about something you could repeat 'I am cool, calm and in control' at least 10 times (*20 is better*) whilst breathing deeply and calmly. The energy created will start to bring about that feeling (*deep breathing also sends more oxygen to the brain.*)

Affirmations can also help dissolve the mental cause of many physical illnesses; they introduce new thought patterns and release the 'dis-ease' in our minds and bodies that exist with old negative thinking patterns. As mentioned earlier, each time we fester on something we are nurturing it, spreading its power, so emotions like guilt, anger, hate, resentment, etc, can turn into a physical illness. We can work to change what we have created by adopting positive affirmations to repeat on a daily basis. One good little book to have around is *Heal your Body* by Louise L. Hay (*an internationally well-known and gifted author*); she provides different affirmations for different problems.

With children it is good to tell them light, magical stories before they go to sleep, feeding and encouraging their imagination to dwell on positive thoughts. Failing time to do this, they can be asked to repeat the words 'nice dreams only' ten times as they go to bed, again, feeding their subconscious with final positive thoughts at the end of each day.

Thoughts are the mind's energy, directly influencing how the physical brain controls the body's physiology. Thought energy can activate or inhibit our body's cell function. This is why I earlier referred to negative thinking or the holding of grudges acting as thought 'toxins' for our cells. The brain controls the behaviour of the body's cells and doctors should not dismiss the power of the mind as something inferior to the power of chemicals and the scalpel. It inevitably disturbs pharmaceutical manufacturers that in most of their clinical trials the placebos, the 'fake' drugs, prove to be as effective as their engineered chemical drugs, this is because the patients 'thought' they would get better, so they did!

The power of the mind is a subject being covered by some mainstream medical researchers and the results suggest that a placebo effect should be seriously considered as an alternative treatment. In a study published in the New England Journal of Medicine, patients were evaluated for debilitating knee pain, then split into groups, one group of patients had surgery and another group had 'fake' surgery where standard incisions were made, the surgeon talked and acted just as he would have done during a real surgery, but did not actually 'do' anything except sew up the incisions after the requisite time had passed. None of the patients involved in the fake surgery were told it was fake but they were monitored. Television news programs graphically illustrated the results where footage showed members of the placebo group walking and playing basketball, doing things they reported they could not do before their 'surgery'. The placebo patients didn't find out for two years that they had fake surgery and one commented, 'In this world anything is possible when you put your mind to it'.

If positive thinking can pull people out of illness and heal a damaged knee, consider what negative thinking can do in our lives!

There is another report of a shoe salesman in the USA suffering from a type of cancer that was, at the time, considered 100 per cent fatal, so it was no surprise when the salesman died a few weeks after his diagnosis. The surprise came after his death when an autopsy found very little cancer in his body, not enough to kill him: he had died with cancer, not from it because he *believed* he was going to die.

My favourite report is the one about a man who, upon finding out he had an incurable cancer, stocked up on food and drink, went home, shut the door and stayed there for two weeks watching videos that made him laugh. On his next visit to the hospital they found that his cancer had reduced in size to one that could be cured! He had laughed himself back to good health! Now this makes sense to me because laughter produces endorphins, which are hormones that are released into our system when we laugh. Endorphins enhance the immune system by activating the natural killer cells which destroy defective cells and cancer cells. Their general effect is to relax tissue so that all the necessary antibodies travel into the affected body region in order to repair and heal. With high endorphin levels in our systems we feel less pain and fewer negative effects of stress.

Let me pause here for a brief interlude. Just take my hand more firmly and let me guide you down a set of steep, winding stone steps which exist in a beautiful wooded area, at the bottom is a natural stone platform and in front of us is a fast flowing stream. We are surrounded and shaded by trees, all we can hear is the soft twittering of birds and the sound of the stream as it runs across the boulders and rocks. On the grassy banks are wild flowers, dotted here and there and above us to the left we can look up and see a small ancient stone bridge which spans the stream. Let us stand here just for a moment to soak-up the tranquillity and absorb the beauty of this scene. Now slowly turn and look behind us, there is water trickling out of a rock into a small pool, attached to the rock is a tin ladle, this is a Wishing Well and this is an introduction to one of my most favourite places in the world, I have been coming to this well since I was 13 years old. (*If you stayed with me on this short journey you would have been using your imagination to picture what I describe, this can be a type of meditation where you can sit and imagine yourself in a place such as this, doing nothing but standing or sitting there drinking in the surroundings and feeling at complete peace.*)

The favourite place I describe is in a country park in Ireland and the wishing well area is one of great natural beauty. The wishing well allows three wishes (*I know three are allowed because the 'old folk' in the nearby town told me so in bygone years.*) When I encounter anyone else at the wishing well I always pass this information on but with the added advice that any wishes to win the lottery may not work, not because I have tried it but because I believe it fulfils wishes based on non-materialistic happiness (*they can always ignore me and wish for the lottery anyway but as it's still peaceful near the well, I guess my advice could be right...chuckles.*)

The first wish I ever made at the well came true the very same day. I had 'wished' to ride a horse and lo and behold that afternoon a local farmer knocked at my aunt's door and asked if my cousin and I would like to ride the horses as they were gathering hay. I stood there 'agog', staring wide-eyed at the farmer as though he was a giant leprechaun, thinking to myself, 'gosh, that was quick!' It remains so to date, every wish I have made at that well has come true, even though I now realise it could be something to do with the fact that I 'believe' in the power of the wishes and when someone truly believes then the reality is attracted into their world. (*Having said that I have a sneaking suspicion that it really is a magical Wishing Well!*)

The reason I am mentioning special places is that when we use the power of our imagination to take ourselves back to moments where we have been at peace or happy, we release endorphins into our bloodstream. Whenever I feel stressed or worried I try to spend five minutes or more visiting that area of my mind that has stored the beauty and peace of the surroundings next to the wishing well. Any memory, which is pleasant, can be used to ease and heal our minds, as our moods and thoughts anchor down into our physical body and general health.

It is good to sit and re-create special moments in our lives, taking them out of the memory banks and putting them down on a list that can be referred to during any down times, acting as self-help medicine for the mind and, from there, the body. The list could consist of top favourite places, people, pets, activities, peak experiences, spiritual figures, flowers, textures, scents and sounds. Just to give an example, my favourite places consist of that wishing well area, our garden in the summer, an old church in the middle of Marbella in Spain, and so on. Activities include spending quality time with family and friends, reading, dancing and walking by the seashore.

Sounds listed embrace the breaking of waves on a seashore, a baby or young child laughing, birds singing the dawn chorus and, most of all, silence!

If you want to study the effect of the natural healer we have within us, one excellent book on the subject is called *The Endorphin Effect* by William Bloom.

Yes, being upbeat, laughing and thinking positively does help our general health but general efforts to think positively do not preclude making observations such as 'it's raining today' or 'a hundred people were killed in the recent earthquake', this is simply saying what is so. Of course, we have to be aware of the world around us, we do not have to close our ears and eyes to everything, we can observe things but need not dwell on them. This is difficult when newspapers and media constantly bombard us with negative happenings around the world, presenting fear and worry; if we took it all too much to heart we would be boarding up our homes, raising the drawbridge and letting the crocodiles out, too frightened to step out into the world at all!

I also suspect those 'powers that be' help create situations by instilling fear into people. 'A recession is coming', the newspapers cry: investors read it, we read it and what happens? A recession! Daily we are bombarded with doom and gloom.

Where are the reports of the good things that are happening and, yes, there are good things going on, from individual people who dedicate their lives to helping others, to visionary leaders of companies who spearhead projects aimed at the welfare of the general public and the environment. They can be found in all areas of life and all countries, but do we hear about them? Not a lot. It might cheer us up and create an air of positivity and expectancy.

For myself, I subscribe to a newspaper called 'Positive News' which details all the good things going on in the world and for me, at least, this serves to balance out the negativities formulated by the majority of the media.

There are many arguments against letting children watch negative, frightening programmes or films, and I am a big advocate for banning the sale of horrific computer games as they serve to desensitise a young person's mind from the horror of playing out that game in real life. No matter how clever the child is, somewhere the violence is making a change in their subconscious; and what of the children of lower intellect, how do they perceive the gory scenes that are part of on their Gameboys or computer?

A recent scientific study at Harvard Medical School took a group of adult volunteers, none of whom could previously play the piano and split them into three groups. The first group were taken into a room with a piano and given intensive piano practise for five days. The second group were taken into an identical room with an identical piano but had nothing to do with the instrument at all. The third group were taken into an identical room with an identical piano and were told that for the next five days they had to just 'imagine' they were practising piano exercises. The results were extraordinary. Not surprisingly, the brains of those who simply sat in the same room as the piano hadn't changed at all. Those who had performed the piano exercises saw marked structural changes in the area of the brain associated with finger movement, but what was really amazing was that the group who had merely imagined doing the piano exercises saw changes in brain structure that were almost as pronounced as those that had actually had lessons!

The power of thought and the power of our imagination is beyond everyday comprehension, but it's real and has a physical basis in our brains, so if something as innocent as imagining piano lessons can bring about a visible physical change in brain structure what changes may come about in a child's mind if they continuously play violent computer games? The cry that 'it's only a game' certainly begins to sound hollow; the same applies to the frightening, gory films some are allowed to watch.

The subconscious mind is a subject worthy of study and there are many good books out there on the subject. One easy informative read is *The Power of the Subconscious Mind* by Joseph Murphy.

Mastering Life

So what is the concluding thought on the subject matter of this chapter?

I guess it is that we have to 'change our minds' by working towards mastering 'it' and ourselves, to evolve to the highest and purest part of our minds.

I set out the following from my heart and address it to you, dear reader, to accept my views as something you may already understand or to reject them, they purely reflect what I have found and believe to be true:

- Always keep an open heart and an open mind.

- Look for ways to connect with your inner self / soul, through meditation or similar practice/study.

- Study and use the knowledge that is available to harness the power of your mind, the possibilities in life rest on the strength of your emotions and imagination.

- Develop your self-belief, strength and willpower to follow your dreams and fly. (do not let the fear of failure stop you stepping forward to realise your dream, for even if   you fail, you had the strength of character to try).

- From a beggar to a king, treat all those who step into your path as equal.

- Besides love, the most important emotion in life is compassion.

- Look 'through' those who come into your life to test your peace of mind, use that emotion of compassion to see that they are not your problem, only their own.

- Embrace positivity, reject negativity.

- Follow your first instinct, your intuition; don't let your mind talk you out of your soul's choice.

- Detach from your ego, it holds you back.

- Know that even in the darkest moment of your life, you are loved in way that you may not fully comprehend right now.

What else is there to say about mastery? Well, I guess mastery is also when you walk around and you're not afraid of life,. It's when you are peaceful when others are not. The situations that would cause drama in others do not in you. It's when the world around you is in chaos yet you walk into it and don't feel chaos, instead, at some level, feeling the wisdom of the ages. It's when somebody yells at you and calls you a name and your first reaction is to wonder if they're right! That is mastery. Our first reaction is to fight back but a master's first reaction is to check him or herself for integrity.

Yes, blessed is he or she who can walk the world in this way whilst spreading the light of the love, goodness and 'God' ness' they possess.

Hold that thought! [smiles].

Know Yourself

Be Who You Are
You are a 'Bright Star',
just a little way to go,
just a few things to know.
You came here from Love,
from our God up above.
What else could you be?
Choose to wake up and see.

Your heart has no fear,
it holds its faith near,
your mind tries too hard
to reason, to guard.
Break free from these chains,
see the love that remains,
it's deep down inside,
let your heart be your guide.

Look to others no more.
Know Yourself' and be sure.
Peace and Joy you will find
in the soul of your mind.
No need now to hide
that special 'You' deep inside,
just Remember Who you Are
You are a Bright Star.

– Patricia M Finn

chapter five

The higher power

As I progressed on my expedition of discovery, immersed in thought and picking up golden nuggets of knowledge along the way, I came across the biggest and brightest jewel of them all. It seemed to have been waiting for me, there, at the crossroads of my life. I didn't recognise the jewel at first until I picked it up and examined it closely, then slowly but surely, the bright light it emitted lit up my soul, lit up my DNA and lit up my mind, erasing all doubt that had formerly lingered there throughout the years. 'So', I thought in wonder, 'it was true then, there is a God!'

The God I had found was not the one I had imagined, up there in the sky, white-to-grey hair with matching beard, sitting on a throne surrounded by angels and cherubs. This God was much, much more, an energy that was incomprehensible, mysterious and something of which we are a part, something that made us all manifestations of this higher source of universal power. I found that our Creator and Infinite Mind is present in every point in space and time, and at every level of creation, being ultimately a divine higher power that is an 'all encompassing love.'

To continue identifying with this energy, Universal Intelligence, Absolute Consciousness, Creator, Infinite Mind and every other description of this Higher Power I will use the word 'God'; this term equals all of the above. I will also use the gender 'Him' or 'He' for simplicity.

How do I now know that God exists? I know our Creator exists as much as I know I will draw my next breath; I know this as much as I know my heart will give the next beat and I will take the next step. It is a deep knowing that exists within many people. We are born knowing God but when we are born, it is like coming down from bright blue skies full of sunshine into clouds of forgetfulness, the clouds stay with us and our memory of God is diminished until we find our own way back to that 'light'.

I do not need God to visit me to prove His existence. Yes, it would make it easy for every soul if He put in an appearance to do a few miracles with an 'I told you so' look, how easy faith would be then! God could have made us like robotic people, hardwired to love and obey him, programming worship into us like a screensaver, but then our compulsory love would be meaningless.

God wants us to love each other and also Him freely, which is one of the many reasons for giving mankind freewill, if there was no challenge for us individually, we would have missed the point of life itself, which is to evolve out of the darkness of man's own creation into the light where this all-encompassing love exists.

I remember reading of a despairing saint who felt that his faith should be acknowledged or recognised in some way. He also felt he was alone and, in despair, he cried out, 'If this is how you treat your friends, God, God help anyone else'. I dwelt upon his dilemma examining in my mind whether any kind of acknowledgement would have helped or should have been forthcoming. Then it struck me that we should not need our faith acknowledged, it is only our haunting ego that needs it. If our faith is strong we do not have to look for signs of recognition from God or higher powers, the natural power and flow of faith will become evident without expectation or want; through faith our soul is growing and rising unbeknown to us.

If we allow ourselves to recognise God or the existence of a Higher Power, we will feel and see that Power all around us; take a look, everything good is God in action, He didn't stop talking to us in biblical times, God still communicates using many means to remind us of what we already know, at soul level.

'God sits and waits for you and me, God sits and waits for us to see, that everything we have is on loan, they lay the path for our way home'. These words popped into my head one day, it is a part of how I see God.

I hope, dear reader, you will allow me to just take a few paragraphs to get on to my soap box and put in a short defence for the bad name God has with some people who are quick to cast blame, on a power they have little faith in, when bad things happen. *I often wonder why such people do not blame the darker forces (if they are thinking in this type of direction).*

Negative happenings emanate from the misuse of the freewill given to mankind. Humanity was given the gift of freewill and the gift of Mother Earth, what have we done with them?

Wars, poverty and hunger are caused by man. There is enough in this world to share, to pass around, but those in power practice greed and 'self' denying their fellow human beings the gifts placed on this earth for us all. In short we do not have to look very far to assess that money and power come before life.

Short-term profit is God to many world banks and major companies, even at the expense of our very existence. The said conglomerates do not give 'a jot' about ordinary people, or how their actions affect the world overall. Look at what they have done to the vast areas of forests that formally acted as a belt around this earth. Trees are an important source of oxygen and they 'eat' carbon dioxide; but none of this matters in the materialistic minds of those individuals in power who care even less about indigenous tribes and animals whose homes they have destroyed.

References are made to global warming being a natural occurrence and disastrous weather conditions being 'freak'; there is no mention of major players who have helped create some of the disasters the world has experienced. One would have to study the hole in the ozone layer which allows the earth to heat up more than it should, causing cracks in the surface which in turn causes tidal waves and other weather extremes, but here and now, I am only touching on this subject, which people are gradually becoming more aware of.

Chemicals and preservatives have been introduced into our food chain for many years with little thought to the fact that our human forms were not built to contend with these unnatural substances. I personally believe that (*as well as the emotion of stress*) many cancers and illnesses are sparked off by additives and hormones that have been put into our food. We live by what we eat and we die by what we eat too.

The lands and seas are poisoned and many species of animals, birds and fish are starting to disappear; I cannot imagine how this earth is going to be in 20 years if all this continues.

Having said this and not meaning to sound too gloomy, it is encouraging to see a shift happening where more people care about the general environment. Some are also demanding better food that is not grown with the help of chemicals or the toxic substances that are injected into the animal flesh we eat; more and more shops and supermarkets are listening to public demand and slowly the worm is turning.

At the moment, a major US company is trying to foist genetically modified, GM, foods on to us all under various guises; I have yet to be convinced that there is a good purpose for its existence and that there will be no long-term consequences. There are studies showing that when humans digest genetically modified foods the artificially created genes transfer into, and alter the character of, the beneficial bacteria in our intestines, so it is apparent that there has not been enough 'honest' research into this subject.

What of the evil which exists, the despots and tyrants of the world who rule through cruelty, fear and oppression of their own kind, their own people? Again, this darkness, hate and greed is 'man-made', a route that is chosen to satisfy the un-evolved selfishness and weaknesses engrained in those individuals involved.

I digress slightly here and but wish to reflect on things which are not 'of God', but 'of Man'. *In my travels I also developed an interest in what was going on in this planet but I will now get off my soapbox, put it to one side and return to the subject of God –* [smiles].

God does not live within the proof system of science or within the limitations of the five senses we are born with.

Humans can only see and hear within a specific frequency band and there are many things around us, that we cannot see or hear but we know they exist. For example, how does science measure the love you feel for your child, partner, parents, and so on? How you feel cannot be measured, you just feel it. Yes, you can see its effects, but you can't 'see' love. You can't see frequencies that travel through the air to operate two-way radios; you can hear the effects but you cannot see the frequency itself, nor can you see the transmitted waves that bring calls to your mobile phones, signals to your television, or the signals that enter and leave the credit card device brought to your table by the waiter. I could go on giving many examples, along with those I formally covered under 'The Meaning of Life' section, but know that you, dear reader, are intelligent enough to work out your own examples of what we have in the air around us that we cannot see.

Using the frequency analogy, God is on a higher frequency that cannot be reached by cold science (*one must also remember that most, not all, but most scientists reflect their own belief systems in their work.*) God can be reached through the heart where the soul who knows and is part of this Higher Power, lives.

You can experience the effects of our Creator, listen to beautiful music, gaze on the wonders of nature, look at someone with love, even in thinking a beautiful thought you will feel the loving power of that Higher Power in action. He has created everything wonderful that you see, hear and feel.

God does not represent fear in any shape or form; you would not fear a loving father who watches you run out into the world creating your own life, whether he approved of what you were doing or not, would you?

As mentioned earlier, in my youth I was introduced to a God who invoked fear, we had to obey Him and do His Will. If you did not follow the Church's teachings, God would condemn you to eternal damnation, causing us to burn in the everlasting fires of hell. This is not the God I found and it is refreshing to find a positive quotation by Pope John Paul II who said the following in Rome on July 28th 1999:

'Damnation cannot be attributed to an initiative of God because in His merciful love he cannot want anything but the salvation of the beings he created. Hell is not an endless fiery torture, Hell does not exist as a place but is a 'situation' in which one finds oneself after freely and definitively withdrawing from God, the source of Life and Joy. The inextinguishable fire and burning oven are 'symbolic' and metaphorical, indicating the complete frustration of a life without God.'

I found a God who loves us all, no matter what choices or mistakes we make, God has the bigger picture and knows that, for everyone 'this' is not all there is, and he waits for us to find the truth of who we really are. Learning through religion can be used as a stepping stone but it is not the only route to God, there are many paths which include finding God in our own way using the gift of intuition as a guide, following a light-filled road avoiding the dark alleys along the way.

God is our Creator and He allows us to be creators, creators of our own lives: we can create our own heaven or our own hell, it is a battle between the heart and the mind, the light and the dark. God wants us to be happy and wants us to have abundance, we do not have to go around in sackcloth and ashes, we can enjoy the fruits of the earth but it is how we use them that measures who we are.

I have seen intelligent individuals denounce the existence of any type of higher consciousness or God but I have also seen no study that they have carried out to reflect their statements apart from references to chosen and carefully selected scientific views or scattered referrals as to why they believe a God does not exist. How do they know? How do I know? It is a belief beyond logic, beyond question, beyond the boundaries of raw science, beyond our five senses, and beyond the human demand for proof.

Higher powers might have a reason to zap someone into line and into belief, as with St. Paul on the road to Damascus, but mostly we are left to find God ourselves, a find that is more precious than all the gold on this material earth.

There are not many people out there who have achieved wealth and fame that can say that money alone brings them lasting happiness. How many end up on drugs in an endless search for something beyond the wealth they have accumulated? Some are evolved enough to use their material wealth to help others and through this they are helping themselves. 'As you give, you will receive': this does not refer to a material return but an inner happiness that radiates naturally when we help others in need.

Many people sense the presence of something they feel is just beyond their reach but when they seek, they find and when they knock, the door is opened, a door that is actually situated in their own minds.

Jesus

W.W.J.D, 'What would Jesus Do?' These are the initials on a small gold bracelet that I wear every day as a gentle reminder to remember His guidance as I face life or problems which may take me out of my present 'awareness' and over to the edge of my emotions. Unlike years ago, I now look at each day as a new day, a chance to try harder, a chance to get it right, a chance to watch my thoughts, words or deeds or 'to turn the other cheek'.

I became closer to Jesus when I unravelled the true meaning of his teachings, hidden behind unfamiliar words, discovering in the process the real person Jesus was: gentle and guiding (*many times misquoted for varying reasons*), he held in his teachings all the secrets of 'The Way'. He pointed us in the direction we needed to go, giving us guidance on how we should think and be in this lifetime if we wished to find our true selves, our souls and in the process find and know God. He showed us what God is like, merciful and kind, he healed the lame and the blind, controlled the movement of fish and calmed storms; not only did Jesus heal many people of sickness and disease, but he raised people from physical death!

Although Jesus walked the earth over 2000 years

ago he remains the most talked about and influential person to have ever lived. Jesus marshalled no army. He didn't write a book or change any laws, so what was his enduring influence?

- More books have been written about Jesus than about any other person in history.

- Nations have used his words as the bedrock of their governments. According to Durant 'the triumph of Christ was the beginning of democracy'.

- The greatest sermon he ever preached was the Sermon on the Mount, which established a new paradigm in ethics and morals.

- Hospitals, schools and humanitarian works have been founded in his name.

- The elevated role of women in Western culture traces its roots back to Jesus. Women in Jesus' day were considered inferior and virtual non-persons until His teachings were followed.

- Slavery was abolished in Britain and America due to Jesus' teaching that each human life is valuable.

- Former drug and alcohol dependents, and others seeking purpose in life, claim Him as the explanation for their changed lives.

- More than two billion people call themselves Christians. Whilst some are Christian in name only, others continue to impact our culture by following Jesus' teachings.

Remarkably, Jesus made all of this impact in just a three-year period. When world historian H.G. Wells was asked who has left the greatest legacy on history, he replied, 'By this test Jesus stands first.'

Those who roll their eyes to the ceiling at the mention of Jesus' name do not seem to comprehend the important part of life that they are missing out on and the knowledge that can be gained. Jesus is not some distant religious figure that is worshipped. Of course, I recognise the divine being Jesus was and is, but I tend to view Him more as a master teacher because the lessons he taught contain everything we need to know on how to evolve as an individual soul

Two of my early poems, *Garden of Peace (one of my favourite ones)* and *Dear Jesus*, reflect my thoughts relating to Jesus. In my earlier years, before my new found awareness, I might have rolled my own eyes to the ceiling if somebody was trying to impress upon me the importance of Jesus' teachings and I often smile at this thought as I look at the screen saver on my mobile phone. Yes, it is a picture of Jesus, a beautiful one, which is shown on the Home page of my website (*and guess whose picture is on my bedside table!*). I'm not sure where the love I hold for Jesus came from, perhaps it is a derivative of the deep respect I hold for Him.

The crucifixion

During my studies on Jesus I went through a period where I told myself that I would not wear a cross, I couldn't understand why Jesus had allowed himself to be killed in such a cruel way, even for the sins of the world.

As I walked further down the path I came to understand that there are many deep meanings behind what Jesus went through. I personally prefer to focus on the joy of the Resurrection, and the way Jesus also demonstrated that even in the most extreme circumstances, where a person is being whipped, beaten, tortured and crucified, it is possible to be loving and forgiving: 'Forgive them father for they know not what they do'. If Christ could do that under those circumstances, I guess we can forgive anything and anyone, *even if we only do this for the sake of our own health and our own minds*.

I also believe that Jesus came for all mankind, not just the few, he came to show us how to walk through our lessons on earth, how to 'be' as God's children and how to find our way 'home'

Garden of Peace

Take my hand and walk with me,
Sit down just here and talk to me,
I'd like to hear what you have to say,
be my lamp, light up the way.

Let us talk of God and Life,
We'll laugh and then we'll smile,
We'll talk of worldly problems,
sit and ponder for a while.

At first I did not understand
the messages that you gave,
I turned my back, I looked away,
one soul you would not save.

But life stepped in with tests for me,
stole the flowers from my mind,
the thorns they hurt but led me back
to your Way, your Truth, your Life.

Sitting here beside you,
soaking up the wisdom of your years,
seeing the Father that you point us to,
wiping away all my former fears.

Dear Jesus, I must go now
but I'll find you again with ease,
sitting here waiting for all Mankind,
in this Beautiful Garden of Peace

– Patricia M Finn

chapter six

Going home

'**D**on't worry Maggie, you're going home'. These were the soothing words my mother heard repeated by her grandfather as she sat holding her grandmother's hand, watching her slowly slip away from this world. My mother was four years old at the time and she told me that this memory has always been held firmly fixed in her mind. At the time she did not understand what her grandfather meant, but in later life realised the truth behind the words. It strikes me now how knowledgeable the old folk were, they seemed to know more than many do these days.

Some people believe that when we die we no longer exist, over and out, dust-to-dust, ashes-to-ashes, and this is correct for those who believe that we are the body and there is nothing else about us or within us to survive. Using my earlier analogy relating to the humble caterpillar, it should be considered possible that all we are doing when our body dies is shedding the vehicle that we have used for our journey on earth, we are greater than our bodies, greater than our minds, we just have to accept that we are more than we think we are.

Death is not to be feared, the only thing to fear is life, having life and not living it, appreciating it, flowing positively with it, experiencing it to the full whilst we walk through it and it need only be in a simple way, one that brings happiness and contentment to our hearts and souls.

There does seem to be a shift in how people now perceive death and more are becoming curious about the possibility that the rumours they have heard through religious sources are true and we are, in fact, eternal. We were, we are and we always will be.

NDE's, Near Death Experiences, have only been a small part of my interest into 'death', but I cover them briefly here because it is something my own father went through. I remember the night I was sitting in the waiting room of my local hospital weeping because my father had undergone a serious operation for peritonitis and we were unsure if he would come through it. I didn't know until later that my father had 'died' during that operation. My father was a quiet, highly intelligent person, not prone to exaggeration, but he told my mother, myself and those close to him that shortly after going under anaesthetic he remembers being drawn towards a bright light. He said he felt so at peace with all, that at that moment, he didn't want to come back. Of course he did, but thereafter he no longer had any fear of death.

I know many nurses and doctors have knowledge of patients who have 'died' and come back to life re-calling different types of experiences that usually involves a bright light and a feeling of peace and love. Those who 'came back' can even remember what the doctors and nurses had said after they passed over, also seeing family and what they were doing in distant places at the time of their deaths, some have recalled going beyond the light into another dimension, recounting what that dimension was like, finding that there are many other levels of reality and that where we live, here on earth, is a pale reflection of our real home. Many doctors have recorded their findings on this subject and there are many books out there on NDEs; it is certainly a subject that is thought provoking and mind boggling.

It is noteworthy also that cold science is proving the existence of an energy above a 'body' after death and I have also looked at the plausible explanations of some who say that NDEs are a product of the closing parts of the mind. however, I haven't seen anything that persuades me this is so, there's too much evidence to the contrary for the open minds who accept the possibility of life after death. Some kind of fear kicks in at the thought of something else/another existence, and this fear turns us from focusing our attention on it, so we come up with plausible excuses to satisfy our sceptical minds.

Many years after my father's eventual death, whilst looking at other areas relating to life and all its complexities, I studied the many layers and opinions on death. I looked at what was said sideways, inside out and upside down, and when I put everything in one big giant jigsaw in my mind, I concluded that there is, in fact, another existence beyond the one we are experiencing, one beyond the body we walk with, one beyond our own awareness and hopes.

It is difficult for us to accept that one day we are all going to leave this earthly existence and I guess many prefer to live in denial of the inevitable. Maybe if we were able to accept that this life is not 'all there is' we might be more open to learning about the process of death itself; it's scary to think about, but we are all going to go through it. Perhaps there will come a time when lessons will be given on what to expect when we 'pass over' and there will be a general acceptance that we need not look at death with such fear or sadness.

It is important to understand how to treat those that are passing from this world, if indeed we are blessed enough to be there at that time. The ideal, of course, is for each of us to die with the company of our loved ones around us, although circumstances may not allow this. Sometimes it is the choice of the departing soul that they wish to leave in peace; other reasons may be that our loved one has been taken by a sudden death of some kind, an accident or other cause where we cannot be with them. *(I found it interesting to find out that a soul can leave the body just before it is about to experience pain or trauma which will cause death to the body.)* Even if we are not present, we can still help them through our prayers, which I shall cover shortly.

If we are able to be with our loved one whilst they are dying they need to hear reassuring words in a peaceful atmosphere, even if they are unconscious. Doctors will agree that we can all hear spoken words at whatever level of consciousness we are in; this includes those who are in a coma. Words should be reassuring, loving and positive, going over good memories and perhaps thanking the loved one for their presence in your life. If the dying process is prolonged, it is good to repeat the same loving words. If surroundings allow it, it would create a calm atmosphere to play soft background music or music the loved one was fond of, ensuring it is not anything 'lively' as everything should remain peaceful.

Consider how it must be for the person lying there for long periods, the music would keep them calm at whatever level of consciousness they are at. Deep grief that is displayed in the presence of someone who is departing does cause that soul anguish that can hold him or her back so it is better to turn to prayer for the loved one if possible.

Along the way I found the following unusual and uplifting prayer in Neale Donald Walsch's book *Home with God*, and I thank him for allowing me to share this with you:

Prayer for those 'Going Home'

The God of your understanding is with you now, even in this hour, at this precise moment, in this place, with you right now, whispering to your soul 'You are welcome, whenever you are ready to come Home'.

You shall not be turned away, not for any cause or reason. If there is a cause or reason you believe to be valid then, God, should you want God to, in this moment, invalidates it. God, should you want God to, in this moment erases it. God, in this moment makes all paths clear, all roads straight, saying 'Make way for my beloved, who chooses to come Home to God'.

This prayer is offered for you, wonderful Being and child of the universe, as you embark on the most joyful journey you have ever taken, filled with wondrous surprises. A journey into the greatest happiness you have ever known and the grandest experience you will ever have.

Dream now of glorious things. Dream of every wish come true. Dream of every pain disappearing, of everything of which time has robbed you being given back to you again. Dream of seeing loved ones once more, all those who have gone before. Know for a certainty that when you leave here you will again be with all those who have held a place in your heart.

And do not worry about those you leave behind, for you will see them too, again and again, and love them, too, again and again, through all eternity as in the present moment, for there can be no separation where there is love, you are eternal and so too are those you love.

Smile then, at the joyful anticipation of what is in store. These gifts have been laid up for you and God has only been waiting for you to return Home to receive them.

Peace, joy and love are you and are yours, now and always. So it is and so it shall be, forever and ever. Amen.

Sad though the parting of a loved one will be, it should be with the acceptance and knowledge that the one who leaves us has only stepped into a waiting world of light. He or she is conscious, safe, not lost, not suffering, they have only passed beyond our immediate vibrational octave, over to another dimension, over to that other reality.

So what happens when we 'die'? Well, my understanding is that, as already mentioned, our soul is the consciousness and power force that we really are and this leaves the body upon death. When we 'pass over' that consciousness expands and we can find ourselves looking down on the scenario we have just left, trying to understand what has happened, although I guess those of us that know and understand the process will have less of a shock!

Just before death, or when the death process is in progress, a bright, clear light may appear and it is helpful if the person involved understands the meaning of the light to ensure they do not miss this opportunity to be guided in the direction they are meant to go, wrapped in the blessing of unimaginable peace. Some souls may be too busy trying to understand what is happening to attach any importance to its presence and lose an opportunity to be helped. However, help can be given in other forms, such as the comforting presence of loved ones who have made this transition before us and have come to show us there is nothing to fear.

We may see no-one and feel as if we are alone, but we can rest assured we are never alone and it helps to hold the knowledge to 'call' for help asking God or a higher being of our choice to help us. With this call help will be given, one way or another whether we understand the process of death or not.

When my maternal grandmother was dying she whispered that she could see my grandfather and her sister Anne who had passed on many years before. In wonder she repeated how well my grandfather was, 'He has no pain', she said. 'He's smiling at me, he looks so young and he's wearing a lovely suit'. Even before I understood what I do now, I realised that something special had happened at that time, she was not having a vision or dream, the clarity of her words were too real

The popular film *Ghost* starring Patrick Swayze must have had spiritually evolved writers as it is based on one version of what can happen when we 'pass over'. At first there is a period of disbelief that we can see everyone around us but they can't see us; the white light appears, initially ignored by the star of the film as he 'wasn't ready to leave'; and, when he was ready, the white light reappeared and he stepped into it.

After we have completed the death process, with the help given and before we 'settle' anywhere, we may find ourselves left alone to view and review our lives, looking over all those ages and stages, viewing the good and the not-so-good actions we took. Armed with our expanded consciousness we will feel remorse for any wrong done. This is a natural process and with remorse comes forgiveness, but first, we must forgive ourselves. We will also feel joy, watching moments where we got life 'right', did the right thing and passed the 'test', in doing so wwe helped our soul to grow.

Of course, there are souls who will remain stubborn, refusing to let go of their earthly minds, regretting nothing, hate or dislike deeply engrained in the darkness they have created in their souls, holding on to how they had become in their lives thus dictating the level of consciousness they will go to next. Such souls do have a bright star within them but it has been covered by the dark fabric of their own minds. However, they do have the potential to raise their awareness towards the light and walk out of the Hell they have created.

I have to stress how important it is for those of us left behind to pray for the person who has passed over, particularly straight after death. Prayers from the heart are always heard and help will be given to the departed from many sources. The power of prayer should never be underestimated, particularly at this time. If someone doesn't know how to pray, i.e. specific prayers, it is fine to just say simple words from the heart, asking for help to be given to the loved one who has departed, love is always heard.

As I drive to work in the morning, I have a favourite prayer, which I regularly say:

Dear Almighty God, Father of All That Is,
May Archangel Michael stay at my right side,
May Archangel Gabriel stay at my left side,
May Archangel Raphael stay in front of me,
and May Archangel Uriel stay behind me,
and above and below me is the loving
presence of God

I also use this prayer for others, whether it is family I am thinking of, for somebody ill or for someone who has or is about to depart from this life, substituting the 'at my right side etc' to the intended recipient's name. It is a wonderful thought to imagine and ask for Archangels to surround you or others who are in need of the help of these divine energies. *(Yes, I do believe in Angels, after all they are mentioned in the bible how many times? Did someone say 400? Perhaps that's another area of research)* [smiles].

Prayer can also be used to assuage the helplessness we feel when we hear or see tragedies happening to others, whoever and wherever they are in this world; it is the one thing we can do to help those involved.

Many people who have lost loved ones often receive a blessing of grace, which sustains them through the grief, and sometimes the person who has passed is able to make their presence known, whether by a 'sense' that they are there or a smell which reminds us of them. Love and concern draws them back to us and I often ponder on how frustrating it must be for them not to be able to communicate with us. One of my first poems is called *Tears to Prayers*. I created this with my loved ones in mind, leaving a message for the day my turn comes to embark upon another fascinating journey. Prayers for loved ones should continue too, remember, prayers equal thoughts, thoughts equal energy, and energy travels, particularly energy from the heart.

Many ask why, if our loved ones 'live on', they can't come back and tell us they are still 'there'. Well, they could if we were born with a dial in our energy that we could use to tune into their new frequency, but the majority of us do not have this ability, so they can only come to us in our dreams when we have 'tuned out' of our conscious minds. There is much I could write on this subject, but the basic fact is that we have to also be allowed to continue our lives to our natural ending. If they were to keep presenting themselves to us, we would remain locked in a world of grief and longing, which would take all of our focus thus creating a scenario where we are unable to complete our journey as an individual soul or let in the natural healing which does come with time. Do not grieve for the loss of a loved one, they are fine; they have crossed the bridge and stepped into another existence, it is us who need help for we will miss their presence in our lives

No one can possibly understand what grief is until they have experienced the loss of a loved one themselves. How can you explain that feeling of emptiness, helplessness and longing? How do you explain how that void feels? It is a sad and difficult time to live through but we can choose to fill that void with knowledge, remembering each moment of each day that 'Love cannot be lost'. It is indelible, it remains a part of us throughout eternity, love becomes grafted on to our souls. Patience and faith will sustain us, accept that those who we have loved will always be with us and we will be with them again when our natural time and turn comes to 'go home'.

Tears to prayers

You know I feel your sorrow,
You know I feel your pain,
You fear that you have lost me
and we will never meet again.

Maybe you think prayers went unheard,
maybe you've lost your faith,
but there is a bigger picture
and your Faith is what it takes.

'Those with Whom We've Walked
in Love, We Will See Again'.
This is God's Divine promise.
See, there really is no end.

Don't grieve for me for you must know
I'm in a bright new dimension
where beauty fills each joyous moment,
way beyond your comprehension.

So Rest In Peace dear Loved One,
change your tears to Prayers.
Know that every one you say for me
sends me Peace beyond compare.

For in Heaven time is nothing,
you'll know one day for sure,
and there is nothing that will keep me
from holding you once more

– Patricia M Finn

chapter seven

The holy grail

As I write this book, my focus is turned to the future, the future of my grandchildren and descendants and what may be in store for them. I am aware that they will have to walk their own walk through life and experience the highs and lows that will be thrown onto their pathway; hopefully they will gather these experiences and use them to create their own strength of character and their own peace of mind. As in my younger years, they may be too busy living their lives to take time out to consider the possibility of the existence of something special within themselves, or to realise the existence of a Higher Power, to this end I hope this book will help them, when they are ready.

If life was perfect. I would create a map. This map would have an 'X', which marks the spot where the treasure is, this is where you will find self-belief and happiness, and this is where that distant, unimaginable and unbelievable 'God' is . But human nature has never really taken the sole view of another easily, so I reign in my words and just sprinkle some curiosity around which will, hopefully, fall on fertile ground.

Maybe I could have expanded upon many of the subjects I cover, but then I would be delving deeper into them and lose you, dear reader, along the way *(is that you dear grandchild, did you feel my nudge to fly?)*. So it is all 'light', just enough to hopefully sow that seed, enough for you to follow the clues given, enough to ponder on the 'what if' scenario, enough to experience the inner joy in finding the treasure yourself.

Only recently I can suddenly see the dreams I reflect on in my simple little poem called *A New World* within reach as there now appears to be so much more promise out there for the future and I believe we are entering an age where a new level of consciousness will prevail.

Knowing that maybe we can blow up this planet a hundred times or more, we will reach the dawn of realisation that we are all here together; then we will unite and say 'We do not need this anymore'. In the new dawn those who operate on a lower, harmful, level of consciousness will be unable to progress with their objectives. After all, darkness is an absence of light, and we each have a powerful light within us that we can shine. One light is bright, but when we join together the light is brilliant; with unity of purpose we will 'put out the dark'.

It is heartening to see that there is an obvious transition occurring where many souls are becoming knowledgeable enough to question what is happening around this world; knowledgeable enough to recognise that we are more than walking, talking human beings and with knowledge and light that new world I talk of is beginning to take shape. It will be a slow process but it is under way; things may get worse before they get better, but better it will certainly get.

I remember watching the victory speech of the US President Barack Obama, on the night he defeated John McCain to become President Elect. Tears streamed down my face as I heard the content of that speech, the audience was caught in a high state of great joy and grown men were crying. If Obama does nothing else in his new presidency, he did, in that speech, in that moment, shift the collective consciousness of all those listening to a higher vibration, a holy vibration where despair at the problems affecting his country and the world melted and changed to Hope. 'Change' and 'Yes, we can' became the mantra creating an exciting energy of positivity and love.

I felt honoured to have watched and lived through a historic moment, which saw the walls of discrimination torn down with Martin Luther King's dream becoming a reality 'Where a black man is judged by the content of his character, not the colour of his skin'. Yes, today, that hope reigns and Obama went into his role with more expectation than any other US President for a long time; only time will tell how successful he will be.

As I look back at the past 12 years I am grateful for the knowledge on life and beyond which I have gained to date. It has brought a lot of peace and understanding into my turbulent mind, even if others do not concur with what I believe it doesn't matter: I am aware that we all have different perspectives. With my personal truth, I view every day happenings differently now, everything seems to make more sense. There is purpose to our lives apart from the ages and stages we all walk through and I rest easy within the divine realisation that:

- Like our own Creator, 'we' are creators and can create a wonderful life if we change our perception about the many things that trouble us.

- There is 'Light' at the end of the tunnel.

- The Holy Grail doesn't exist 'outside of us'; it sits and waits, dormant, shining, beckoning in all its glory, within each one of us.

Mankind has galloped across the Millennium of time searching for the world's greatest secret in caves, under ancient stones, temples and churches looking for the Holy Grail, convinced it held the secret of life, the realisation didn't dawn on them that the Holy Grail is really a metaphor.

Should you, dear reader, manage to find your own Holy Grail, grasp it with both of your hands and through the eyes of your heart, take a look inside, there within the sparkling bright light and mist you will see smiling back at you – your own reflection!

A New World

A New World is coming,
it's emerging through the mist,
hold on to Faith, Hope and Love,
we're next on Heaven's List.
The King will be full balance,
freedom and food for All
The Queen will be unity
No fighting and no war

Mother will be Planet Earth,
with joy she'll spin around,
knowing her air, seas and land
are clean, are safe and sound.
Father will be ticking time
in eternity he'll suspend
retirement of his moving parts
in a world that has no end.

The Children will be mankind,
brown, yellow, black and white,
selfless thoughts, words & deeds,
evolved in knowledge and light.
Creatures, they'll all live in peace,
no prey or man to fear,
grazing on all nature's gifts
in Earth's new atmosphere.

Yes, New World is coming,
see it emerging through the mist,
hold on to all the faith you have,
we're next on heaven's list.

– Patricia M Finn

Epilogue

Before I sign off, I would like to share with you the inspiring quotations that I collected along my journey, little nuggets of wisdom that served to light up some part of my soul. I always carried a little battered notebook with me and when something popped into my mind or I came across a positive quotation I liked, I would record it, hungry to remember the insight expressed. I did not record all the authors as there were so many books involved but I start with the ones I did record. I feel these quotations fit well with the thoughts I reflect upon throughout this book.

> Darkness cannot drive out darkness,
> only light can do that.
> Hate cannot drive out hate,
> only love can do that
> *Dr Martin Luther King Jnr*

♥

To conquer oneself is a greater task than
conquering others
Buddha

The important thing is to not stop questioning
Albert Einstein

The Kingdom of God is within you
Jesus

An eye for an eye only makes the whole world blind
Mahatma Gandhi

We can easily forgive a child who is afraid of the dark,
the real tragedy of life is when men are afraid
of the light
Plato

Know thyself
Socrates

The source of negativity can be overcome
through the energy of love

Find silence if you want wisdom
for within silence wisdom speaks

Do not measure yourself by other peoples measuring
sticks, this is your life, create your own sense of worth
and recognise both the good and not so good in you,
recognition is a step forward.

If we understood the power of our thoughts,
we would guard them more closely. If we understood
the huge / awesome power of our words we would
prefer silence to anything negative.

We are here to help and care for each other
Without love in our hearts and souls, we are nothing.

♥

What distorts many people is a lack of love.

Do not look down and condemn any man for their weakness, take their hand, give them hope and something to strive for, with faith they will respond.

There are no tricks, short cuts or gimmicks to get to 'heaven', the path is Pure and Simple.

Life is laughter and tears, delight and defeat, joy and sorrow a path of learning we must walk. Meet every struggle with strength and every success with humility.

You may feel you know everything, but do you know yourself? Would you recognise your soul in the dark?

Become a warrior of life, using Wisdom as armour, Knowledge as a shield and Truth as your shining sword.

As a warrior fight no others but fight your own conditioning, your own hormones, and your own weaknesses.

Understand the law of 'Cause and Effect'.

We can too often be deceived by outer appearances.

Encountering and overcoming obstacles is growth opportunity for yourself and your soul, always choose the kind / wise / loving solution.

Never criticize, condemn, gossip or say an unkind word against another, nor harbour hatred, resentment or revenge, all are tools that darken the soul.

If people have no inner peace how are they to find it outside of themselves?

Find your own faith through study, see what your soul recognises and what it rejects.

Knowledge is Light
(Your soul cannot grow if it doesn't know)

Do not look for your identity in the way others
respond to you.

We feed our bodies and we can also feed our souls
with prayers, positive thoughts,
words and deeds.

We all have choices in life; we can choose to be kind
or cruel, forgiving or vengeful, generous or miserly,
compassionate or judgemental, what do you choose?

The strongest poison to the human spirit is the
inability to forgive yourself or another person.

Forget bad experiences in life,
to forgive is not to condone.

Interpret all situations and relationships as having a symbolic importance even if you can't immediately understand what it is.

Do not keep seeking advice from others; listen to your own intuition, this is your true guide.

The most valuable thing in life is your soul,
What if you gain the whole world but lose your own eternal soul in the process?

Gather not the treasures of life, which will rust and decay, gather the treasure of your soul that never decays and is eternal.

Why worry when you can pray?

The closer you get to God the harder is the work for the devil.

When you make a mistake, stop and gain the
golden nugget of wisdom, learn the lesson,
forgive yourself and stride forward.

When unsure of what to do ask
'What would Jesus Do?'

It is easy to extend love when everything is well,
the test is to extend love when chaos exists.

Negative happenings do not come from God,
they come from humanity's misuse of freewill.

The most important relationship in your life
is with yourself.

♥

Emit your own frequency of Love rather than
absorbing the frequencies around you.

♥

If you stand strong in your chosen belief
you should not feel the need to suppress
someone else's ideas or religion.

As long as you face the light,
the shadows are always behind you.

Truth feels as if you already know it.

Ignore voices of fear and negativity, the less you
energise them with the power of your attention
the more rapidly they will fade.

Do nothing that does not bring you peace.

Most people refuse to believe what they do not
understand.

God lives outside of our five senses.

Everywhere you look God is there.
Your can see a part of God in every face,
you can hear the voice of God in every river,
there is nowhere God does not exist.

Life is the breath of God

We are not apart from God, God is a part of us.

Look at everything God created with Love,
including yourself.

♥

Life is eternal and death is only a horizon and a
horizon is nothing save the limit of our sight.

♥

To order further copies of

Divine Realisation
– One Soul's Journey

Please visit website:

www.solbooks.co.uk

or

send the coupon on the next page by post

To: S.O.L. Books, PO Box 280, St. Neots PE19 9ED

Divine Realisation – One Soul's Journey

Please send me **one** copy for £6.99 (€8.75, $11.75)	

or save money by ordering two copies or more:

Send .... additional copies for £5.99 (€7.50, $10.25)	
Postage/pack: £2.50 first book + £1 each additional book (€3.00 first book + €1.50 each additional book, $3.50 first book + $3 each additional book)	
Payment enclosed: Cheque / Money Order payable to S.O.L. Books	

Print name: ....

Address: ....

....

.... Post Code / Zip: ....

Tel No: ....

Email: ....

The poems in this book and other poems, as shown on the above website, are also available to order as laminated bookmarks. See overleaf and Website **www.solbooks.co.uk** for details.

We do not share or sell our customers' details.

To: S.O.L. Books, PO Box 280, St. Neots PE19 9ED

Poems – Laminated Bookmarks

Please send me the following bookmarks.
(These can be viewed online at **www.divinerealisation.co.uk**
where poems not shown below can also be ordered.)
I understand the minimum quantity to order is 5.

Please send a set of 5 poems at £3.75 per set, my choice is ticked below. (€4.50, $6.50)	
Send .... additional poem/s for £0.75 each (€0.90, $1.25)	
Postage per set of 5 = £0.50 (€0.60, $0.90)	
Payment enclosed: Cheque / Money Order payable to S.O.L. Books	

Enter quantity required (minimum of 5)

Thank You .... Beacon of Light ....

Medicine for Inner Happiness ....

Know Yourself .... Garden of Peace ....

Tears to Prayers .... A New World ....

Print name: ....

Address: ....

....

.... Post Code / Zip: ....

Tel No: ....

Email: ....

We do not share or sell our customers' details.

The Author of

Divine
Realisation

One Soul's Journey

can be contacted

at

www.divinerealisation.co.uk

About the author

For over 25 years, Patricia Finn has been a company executive director for a small successful company, working in communication technologies, based in Cambridgeshire, U.K.. Her role embraces many differing duties, the main one being within the Personnel / Human Resources  Department where she finds this aspect of her job to be both the most enjoyable and the most challenging.

Patricia's intention, when writing *Divine Realisation – One Soul's Journey*, was to keep it as a record for her grandchildren to view in the future, however, after sending copies of an early version out to family members (as a small gift at Christmas) she was encouraged, by the varying responses she received, to address the book to a wider audience.